HMH |  into **Readi**

M000237734

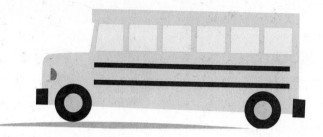

myBook

· ·

GRADE K

Printed in the U.S.A.

ISBN 978-0-358-44925-6

8 9 10 11 12 13 14   0877   28 27 26 25 24 23

4500863090

r1.21

Contents

The **characters** are the people, animals, or creatures in a story.

The **setting** is where and when the story takes place.

✏ Draw a picture of the characters in *Keisha Ann Can!*

✏ Draw a picture of the setting in *Keisha Ann Can!*

Keisha Ann can do many things at school.
What can you do at school?

 Draw a picture of something you do at school.

Write a sentence to tell what you do at school.

BIG IDEA WORDS

Use Big Idea Words to talk and write about a topic.

✔️ Pick one sentence.

partners

☐ I will **discover** how to ____ at school.

☐ One **dream** I have is to ____.

☐ We work with **partners** when we ____.

✏️ Draw a picture to show your response.

The **plot** is what happens at the beginning, middle, and end of a story.

 Draw what happens at the beginning, middle, and end of *A Squiggly Story*.

Beginning

Middle

End

We read about people, places, and things in *One Happy Classroom*. What do you see in your school or classroom?

 Draw a picture of people, places, or things you see in your school or classroom.

Write a label that tells how many people, places, or things are in your picture.

Pictures can give us clues about the meaning of an unknown word.

Listen to the sentence.

Color the part of the picture that shows the <u>underlined</u> word.

Tell your partner the meaning of the <u>underlined</u> word.

1. My teacher shakes a **tambourine** when we sing during music.

2. I use a **quilt** on my bed to stay warm when it's cold out.

3. Raul uses the rake to make a **pile** of leaves.

4. Ella grabbed her umbrella to stay dry from the **precipitation**!

Poems can have **rhythm** and **rhyme**.

- **Rhythm** is the beat or pattern of a poem.

- Words that **rhyme** have the same end sound.

👂 Clap the rhythm of the poem.

✏️ Draw a picture of the word that rhymes.

fine

☐ look

☐ line

blue

☐ two

☐ cups

tune

☐ note

☐ afternoon

The children in *School Day* take school buses to school. How do you get to school?

✏️ Draw a picture of how you get to school.

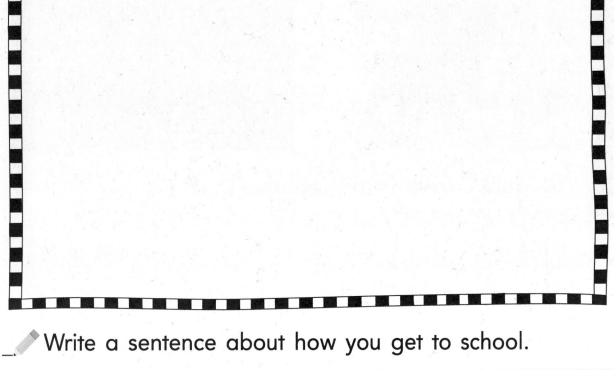

✏️ Write a sentence about how you get to school.

_____

- -

_____

_____

- -

_____

_____

- -

_____

Other words can give clues about the meaning of an unknown word.

🔊 Listen to the sentence for clues.

⭕ Circle the picture that shows the meaning of the <u>underlined</u> word.

1. The horses are in the <u>shade</u> under the tree.

2. The ducks swim in the <u>pond</u>.

3. The <u>toucan</u> lands on a branch.

The **topic** is what a text is about in one or two words.

The **central idea** is the most important idea in the text.

Write the topic of *Schools Around the World*.

_____

- - - - - - - - - - - - - - - - - -

_____

Write or draw the central idea.

We read about many different types of schools in *Schools Around the World*. What words describe your school?

Draw a picture of your school.

Write words that describe your school.

_____

- - - - - - - - - - - - - - - - - - -

_____

- - - - - - - - - - - - - - - - - - -

_____

- - - - - - - - - - - - - - - - - - -

Pictures and other words can give us clues about the meaning of an unknown word.

 Listen to the sentence for clues.

Color in the picture that shows the meaning of the <u>underlined</u> word.

1. The <u>**wallaby**</u> uses its big feet to jump and its long tail for balance.

- -

2. The flower's long <u>**stalk**</u> helps it grow big and tall.

- -

3. I used a pencil to <u>**sketch**</u> a picture of my family during art.

The **problem** in a story is something that goes wrong or causes trouble.

The **solution** is the way the problem is fixed or solved.

 Draw the problem in *I Am René, the Boy.*

Problem

 Draw the solution in *I Am René, the Boy.*

Solution

René shares ideas about how his name is special.
What ideas can you share about how your name is special?

Write your name.

Draw or write two ideas that show how your name is special.

Module 2 • Week 1

Use Big Idea Words to talk and write about a topic.

✔ Pick one sentence.

☐ I **celebrate** ____.

☐ I see lots of **different** ____ outside.

☐ I am **special** because I ____.

✏ Draw a picture to show your response.

special

The **topic** is what a text is about in one or two words.
The **theme** of a story is the message or lesson the
author wants the reader to learn.

 Write the topic of *I Like Myself!*

_____

- -

_____

Write the theme of *I Like Myself!*

_____

- -

_____

_____

- -

_____

Draw a picture of the girl.

The animals in *ABC I Like Me!* share why they feel good about themselves. What makes you feel good about you?

Write what makes you feel good about you.

_____

- -

_____

Write the letter that starts your word and draw a picture.

SYNONYMS AND ANTONYMS

Antonyms are words with opposite meanings.

 Color the picture of the word that is an antonym of the <u>underlined</u> word.

hot   cold

1. <u>quiet</u>   loud   silent

2. <u>small</u>   tiny   huge

3. <u>laugh</u>   frown   giggle

4. <u>light</u>   dark   bright

The **problem** in a story is something that goes wrong or causes trouble.

The **solution** is how the problem is fixed or solved.

 Draw the problem in *Snail & Worm Again.*

Problem

 Draw the solution in *Snail & Worm Again.*

Solution

Pete the Cat wears outfits that make him feel happy.
What outfit makes you feel happy?

Draw a picture of an outfit that makes you feel happy.

Label your clothes. Tell what color they are.

Synonyms are words with the same meaning.

✏️ Color the picture of the word that is a synonym of the <u>underlined</u> word.

happy   glad

1. <u>watch</u>   look   sleep

2. <u>sad</u>   upset   happy

3. <u>near</u>   close   far

4. <u>scared</u>   bored   afraid

The **theme** of a story is the message or lesson the author wants the reader to learn.

✎ Write the theme of *Tiny Rabbit's Big Wish*.

_____

- -

_____

- -

_____

- -

_____

✎ Draw tiny rabbit at the end of the story.

Tiny rabbit's big ears make him special. What makes you special?

Write a sentence that tells what makes you special.

_____

- -

I am special because I _____

_____

- -

_____

Draw a picture of what makes you special.

Synonyms are words with the same meaning.

fast   quick

Antonyms are words with opposite meanings.

slow   fast

⭕ Circle the word that is a synonym of the <u>underlined</u> word.

✏️ Draw a square around the word that is an antonym of the <u>underlined</u> word.

1. <u>tired</u>   sleepy   awake

2. <u>clean</u>   neat   messy

3. <u>wet</u>   dry   soaked

The **central idea** is the most important idea in a text.
Key details are facts or examples that give more information about the central idea.

Draw or write three key details that support the central idea in *Places in My Community*.

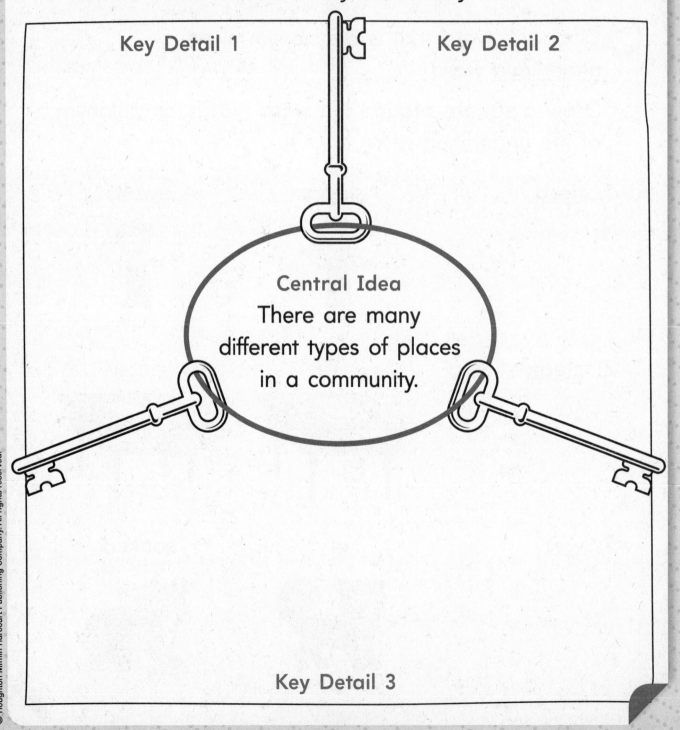

Key Detail 1

Key Detail 2

Central Idea
There are many different types of places in a community.

Key Detail 3

The girl made a map of her neighborhood for her grandma. Can you make a map of your classroom?

Draw a map of your classroom. Use symbols to show special places.

Make a key that tells what the symbols stand for.

Use Big Idea Words to talk and write about a topic.

✔ Pick one sentence.

community

☐ One place in my **community** is ____.

☐ The **location** of my school is ____.

☐ My **neighbor** is ____.

✏ Draw a picture to show your response.

DESCRIBE CHARACTERS

Characters are the people, animals, or creatures in a story.
Picture and text clues describe what characters say, think, and do.

✏️ Draw a picture of each character.

✏️ Write words that describe each character.

Tita

Mr. Gómez

Quinito

We spotted hidden letters in *ABC: The Alphabet from the Sky.*
Where do you see a hidden letter in the classroom?

✏️ Draw a hidden letter in the classroom.

✏️ Write directions to help readers find the letter,
like: Can you spot the A?

_____

- -

_____

_____

- -

_____

We can sort words and objects into groups.

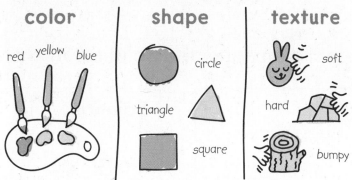

color   shape   texture

Sort the objects into groups by shape.

| baseball | sandwich | gift | tire | window |

CIRCLE ●	SQUARE ■	TRIANGLE ▲

The **theme** of a story is the message or lesson the author wants the reader to learn.

 Draw the problem and the solution in the story.

Problem	Solution

Write or draw the theme of *A Bucket of Blessings*.

Theme

Bo and Peter are best friends. They do many things together. What do you like to do with your friends?

Draw something you and your friend like to do together.

Write about what you and your friend like to do together.

_____

We like to _____

_____

Module 3 • Week 3

SORTING AND GROUPING

We can sort words and objects into groups.

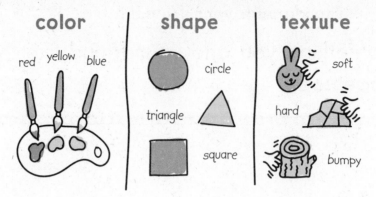

color   shape   texture

red yellow blue

circle

triangle

square

soft

hard

bumpy

Sort the activities into things Bo and Peter do indoors and things they do outdoors.

splash in the water	draw dinosaurs
read books	look for frogs
make sand castles	play ball

INDOOR ACTIVITIES	OUTDOOR ACTIVITIES

Characters are the people, animals, or creatures in a story. Picture and text clues describe what characters say, think, and do.

🖋 Write or draw what Hee Jun says, thinks, and does in the beginning, middle, and end of the story.

> **Beginning: Hee Jun in Korea**

> **Middle: Hee Jun in West Virginia**

> **End: Hee Jun in West Virginia**

Homes can come in all shapes and sizes.
What does your "Home Sweet Home" look like?

✏️ Draw a picture of your "Home Sweet Home."

✏️ Write words that describe your "Home Sweet Home."

We can sort words and objects into groups.

color

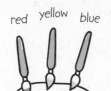

red   yellow   blue

shape

circle

triangle

square

texture

soft

hard

bumpy

✎ Sort the homes into groups.

HOMES THAT CAN MOVE		HOMES THAT CAN NOT MOVE

Module 3 • Week 4

The **central idea** is the most important idea in a text.
Key details are facts or examples that give more information about the central idea.

Draw or write two key details that support the central idea in *Being Fit*.

Key Detail 1

Central Idea
There are many things you can do to be fit.

Key Detail 2

There are many activities you can do to be fit and healthy.
What do you do to be fit and healthy?

Draw a picture showing what you do to be healthy.

Write a sentence about what you do to be healthy.

BIG IDEA WORDS

Use Big Idea Words to talk and write about a topic.

✓ Pick one sentence.

☐ I have **energy** after I ____.

☐ One way to **exercise** is to ____.

☐ One **healthy** snack is ____.

energy

✏ Draw a picture to show your response.

The **central idea** is the most important idea in a text.
Key details are facts or examples that give more information about the central idea.

✏️ Draw or write three key details that support the central idea in *Get Up and Go!*

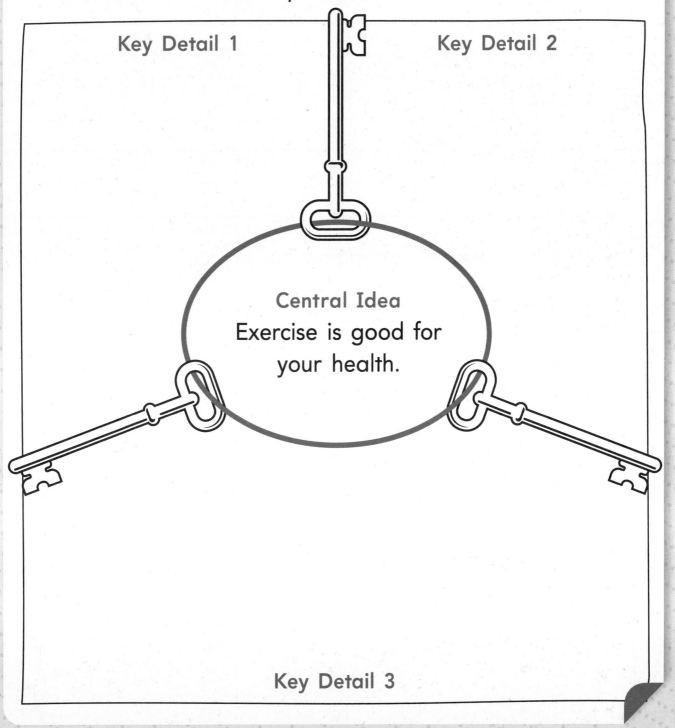

Key Detail 1

Key Detail 2

Central Idea
Exercise is good for your health.

Key Detail 3

Animals and people can stretch in many different ways.
What is one way you can stretch?

Write a sentence about a way you can stretch.

Draw a picture of you doing the stretch.

We can put similar words in order of meaning.

actions

jog   run   sprint

Write the action words from smallest to biggest.

Draw a picture to go with each word.

jump	leap	hop

smallest   BIGGEST

The **plot** is what happens in a story. When we retell a story, we tell the characters, setting, and main events.

✎ Draw or write what happens in the beginning, middle, and end of *Jack & the Hungry Giant*.

Beginning

Middle

End

Fruits and vegetables come in all the colors of the rainbow!
What new fruit or vegetable do you want to try?

Write a sentence about a new fruit or vegetable you want to try. Include its color!

_____

- -

_____

_____

- -

_____

_____

- -

_____

Draw a picture of you eating the fruit or vegetable you want to try.

We can put similar words in order of meaning.

little

tiny

teeny

✏ Write the size words from smallest to biggest.

✏ Draw a picture to go with each word.

huge	giant	big

smallest

BIGGEST

The **central idea** is the most important idea in a text. **Key details** are facts or examples that give more information about the central idea.

Draw or write three or four key details that support the central idea in *Getting Rest.*

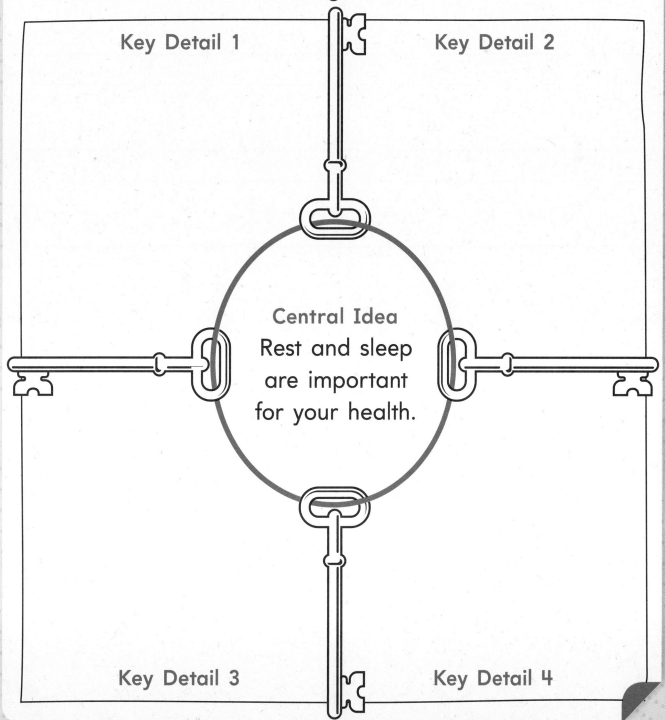

Key Detail 1

Key Detail 2

Central Idea
Rest and sleep are important for your health.

Key Detail 3

Key Detail 4

There are many ways you can help your body get ready to sleep. What do you do to get ready to go to sleep?

Write a sentence about one way you get ready to sleep.

_____

_____

_____

_____

Draw a picture showing how you get ready to sleep.

We can put similar words in order of meaning.

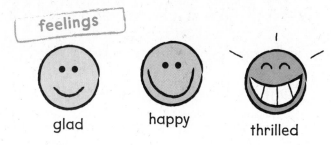

feelings

glad   happy   thrilled

Write the words in order from least active to most active.

| sleepy | active | calm | relaxed | energized |

Characters are the people, animals, or creatures in a story. Picture and text clues tell how a character feels.

✏️ Draw Jabari's face. Show how he feels.

✏️ Write words that tell how Jabari feels.

Beginning

Middle

End

READING RESPONSE

Little Critter can do many things by himself. What can you do?

Draw a picture showing something you can do.

Write a sentence about something you can do.

Use Big Idea Words to talk and write about a topic.

✔ Pick one sentence.

☐ It takes **practice** to _____.

☐ I feel **proud** that I can _____.

☐ One **success** I had at school was learning to _____.

proud

✏ Draw a picture to show your response.

Character traits are words that describe a character.
Make **inferences** to identify character traits.

✎ Draw the Little Red Hen's friends at the beginning and end of the story.

✎ Write the character traits of the friends at the beginning and end of the story.

In the beginning, the Little Red Hen's friends are

_____

_____

_____

In the end, the Little Red Hen's friends are

_____

_____

_____

We can make connections between two versions of the same story to think about what is the same and what is different.

✎ Write or draw things that are different in the top and bottom.

✎ Write or draw things that are the same in the middle.

The Little Red Hen (Makes a Pizza)

Both Stories

The Little Red Hen On Stage

MULTIPLE-MEANING WORDS

Some words have more than one meaning.

wave

Listen to each sentence for meaning clues.

Draw a picture that shows the correct meaning of *trunk*.

The elephant uses its <u>trunk</u> to grab food.

I put my backpack in the <u>trunk</u> of the car.

The **problem** in a story is something that goes wrong or causes trouble.

The **solution** is the way the problem is fixed or solved.

 Draw the problem in *Ish*.

> Problem

 Draw the solution in *Ish*.

> Solution

Ramon loves to draw. What do you love to do?

Draw a picture of you doing something you love.

Write a sentence about something you love to do.

_____

- -

_____

- -

_____

- -

_____

Some words have more than one meaning.

✏️ Draw a picture to show another meaning for each word.

⭕ Circle the picture that shows the meaning of the word in the sentence.

bat

bowl

I like to **bowl** with my friends.

duck

There was only one **duck** at the park.

The **topic** is what a text is about in one or two words.
The **theme** of a story is the message or lesson the author wants the reader to learn.

✏️ Write the topic of *Emmanuel's Dream.*

_____

_____

✏️ Write the theme of *Emmanuel's Dream.*

_____

_____

_____

✏️ Draw a picture of Emmanuel at the end of his ride.

READING RESPONSE

The girl in the story learned to ride a bicycle.
What is something you learned how to do?

✎ Write a sentence about something you learned to do.

_____

- -

I learned how to _____

_____

- -

_____

✎ Write and draw each step.

First	
Next	
Last	

Some words have more than one meaning.
We can look up word meanings in a dictionary.

hard

 Look up both meanings of **watch** in a dictionary.

 Draw a picture of each meaning.

Choose one meaning and write a sentence.

The **illustrations** in a book show the meaning of the text.
They help us understand the text better.

✓ Pick a line of text from *America the Beautiful*.

☐ "For amber waves of grain"

☐ "For purple mountain majesties"

☐ "From sea to shining sea!"

Draw a picture to show the meaning of the text.

There are many different places in our country.
What is one type of place in our country?

✏️ Write a sentence about a place in our country.

_____

- - - - - - - - - - - - - - - - - - - -

In our country, there are _____

_____

- - - - - - - - - - - - - - - - - - - -

_____

✏️ Draw a picture of the place.

Module 6 • Week 1

Use Big Idea Words to talk and write about a topic.

country

✔ Pick one sentence.

☐ One **country** I want to visit is ____

☐ One group I **belong** to is ____.

☐ In school, I have the **right** to ____.

✏ Draw a picture to show your response.

The **author's purpose** is the reason why the author writes a text. Sometimes, the author might have more than one purpose!

✔ Check the author's purposes for writing *Take Me Out to the Yakyu.*

☐ **Persuade**   ☐ **Inform**   ☐ **Entertain**

✏ Draw something you learned about baseball in America and yakyu in Japan.

Baseball in America	Yakyu in Japan

READING RESPONSE

We can make connections between ideas in a text to think about what is the same and what is different.

✎ Write or draw things that are different in the top and bottom.

✎ Write or draw things that are the same in the middle.

Baseball in America

Both Countries

Yakyu in Japan

An *–s* at the end of a noun tells us there is more than one thing.

Look inside the word. ➡ | base|ball|s |

✏ Write an *s* at the end of the word if there is more than one thing.

✏ Draw the number of things listed.

1. 1 star____	
2. 2 book____	
3. 1 hat____	
4. 5 bug____	

Module 6 • Week 2

The **author's purpose** is the reason why an author writes a text. Sometimes, the author writes the text in a way that makes it easier to persuade, inform, or entertain the reader.

✔ Check the author's purpose for writing *Martin Luther King, Jr.*

☐ **Persuade**   ☐ **Inform**   ☐ **Entertain**

✎ Draw or write something you learned about Dr. King.

The president of the U.S. has many jobs.
What is one fact you learned about a U.S. president?

✎ Write a fact you learned.

_____

- -

_____

_____

- -

_____

_____

- -

_____

✎ Draw a picture that goes with your fact.

MEANING CLUES

Use word parts at the beginning or end of words as meaning clues.

Meaning Clues	
Beginning of Word	**End of Word**
re = again *un* = not *pre* = before	*ed* = already happened *ful* = full of

◯ Circle the meaning clue in the word.

✏ Use the clue to write the word meaning.

Word	Word Meaning
r e t e l l	to tell _____
u n h a p p y	_____ happy
p r e p a y	to pay _____
j u m p e d	_____ jumped
c o l o r f u l	_____ color

Authors use words to help readers **visualize** using the five senses:

sight	sound	smell	touch	taste

○ Circle the sense that you use when you picture the text.

✏ Draw a picture of what you visualize.

sight sound smell touch taste	"I hear the parade—*BOOM, BOOM, BOOM.*"

sight sound smell touch taste	"The noodles feel like shoelaces."

Everyone celebrates the Fourth of July in different ways. How do you celebrate the Fourth of July?

✏️ Write a sentence to tell how you celebrate.

_____

- -

On the Fourth of July, _____

_____

- -

_____

✏️ Draw a picture to show how you celebrate.

Compound words are words made up of two words.

Look inside the word.

base|ball|s

✏️ Make a line between the two words in each compound word.

✏️ Draw a picture to show what each compound word means.

t o o t h b r u s h	**b a c k p a c k**
g o l d f i s h	**p o p c o r n**

DESCRIBE SETTING

The **setting** is where and when a story takes place. It can change from the beginning, to the middle, to the end of a story.

✏️ Draw or write words to describe the setting at the beginning, middle, and end of the story.

Beginning

Middle

End

The rabbit imagined the box to be many different things.
What can you make the box into?

✏️ Draw a picture of you and your "Not-a-box."

✏️ Write a sentence to tell what your "Not-a-box" is.

_____

_____

It's not a box! It's a _____

_____

_____

Use Big Idea Words to talk and write about a topic.

✔ Pick one sentence.

☐ I like to **watch** ____.

☐ Something I **wonder** about is ____.

☐ One place in the **world** I want
to go is ____.

watch

✏ Draw a picture to show your response.

The **setting** is where and when a story takes place.
Picture and text clues describe the setting.

Write words to describe how the setting
looks, sounds, and feels.

Looks

Sounds

Feels

Draw the setting in *I Know the River Loves Me*.

The girl in *I Know the River Loves Me* loves to be at the river. Where is your favorite place to be?

Draw a picture of your favorite place.

Write words on your picture that show what you see, hear, smell, or feel at your favorite place.

We can put similar words in order of meaning.

actions

jog   run   sprint

Write the words below in order from smallest action to biggest action.

bite	nibble	chomp	chew

SMALLEST ACTION

BIGGEST ACTION

The **illustrations** in a book show the meaning of the text. They help us understand the text better and make reading more fun.

✔ Pick a line of text from *Me . . . Jane*.

☐ "She cherished Jubilee and took him everywhere she went. And Jane loved to be outside."

☐ "Jane learned all she could about the animals and plants she studied in her backyard and read about in books."

☐ "Jane dreamed of a life in Africa, too."

✏ Draw a picture to show the meaning of the text.

We learned many things about Dr. Jane Goodall.
What is one thing you learned about her?

✏ Write a sentence about Dr. Jane Goodall.

_____

- -

_____

_____

- -

_____

_____

- -

_____

✏ Draw a picture of Dr. Jane Goodall.

We can put similar words in order of meaning.

actions

jog   run   sprint

Write the words below in order from loudest laugh to quietest laugh.

| roar | giggle | laugh | chuckle |

LOUDEST LAUGH

_____

- - - - - - - - - - - - - -

_____

_____

- - - - - - - - - - - - - -

_____

_____

- - - - - - - - - - - - - -

_____

_____

- - - - - - - - - - - - - -

_____

QUIETEST LAUGH

An **opinion** is what someone feels or thinks about something.
A **reason** is why someone feels or thinks a certain way
about something.

Draw a line to match the character to the opinion.

Character	Opinion
Boy	Let the ant live.
Ant	Squish the ant.

Draw pictures to show the boy's and
the ant's reasons.

The boy thinks . . .

The ant thinks . . .

The ant tried to persuade the boy not to squish him.
Would you squish the ant? Why or why not?

✔ Check your opinion.

☐ I would squish
   the ant.

☐ I would not squish
   the ant.

✏ Write a reason for your opinion.

_____

- -

_____

- -

_____

_____

- -

_____

✏ Draw a picture that shows what you would do.

We can put similar words in order of meaning.

feelings

glad   happy   thrilled

Write the words below in order from least wet to most wet.

| damp | wet | soaked | soggy |

LEAST WET

_____

_____

_____

_____

MOST WET

Authors tell events or steps in the order they happen.
When we **retell events in order**, we use signal words like
first, *next*, *then*, and *last*.

✏️ Write signal words to tell the order of each step.

✏️ Draw a picture to show each step.

_____

- - - - - - - - - - - - - - - - -

_____ ,

the fruit falls from the tree.

_____

- - - - - - - - - - - - - - - - -

_____ ,

the fruit opens.

_____

- - - - - - - - - - - - - - - - -

_____ ,

the shell opens.

_____

- - - - - - - - - - - - - - - - -

_____ ,

the walnut is ready to eat.

Plants feed us! How does a seed become a plant?

✏️ Draw a picture of each step.

✏️ Write a sentence for each step. Use signal words like *first*, *next*, *then*, and *last*.

Module 8 • Week 1

BIG IDEA WORDS

Use Big Idea Words to talk and write about a topic.

✓ Pick one sentence.

☐ You can grow ____ in a **garden**.

harvest

☐ You **harvest** fruits or vegetables when they are ____.

☐ After you **plant** a seed, you need to ____.

✏ Draw a picture to show your response.

SAME AND DIFFERENT

We can think about what is the **same** and what is **different** about the two **settings**: up in the garden and down in the dirt.

✏️ Draw a picture of what happens up in the garden and down in the dirt.

Up in the Garden	
Down in the Dirt	

✔️ Is what's happening the same or different?

☐ **Same**   ☐ **Different**

Many people think earthworms are icky! But earthworms are important for the soil. What did you learn about earthworms?

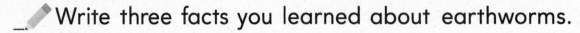 Write three facts you learned about earthworms.

 Draw pictures of earthworms on your fun facts page.

Fun Facts about Earthworms!

1.

2.

3.

MULTIPLE-MEANING WORDS

Some words have more than one meaning.

✎ Draw a picture that shows the meaning of each word as a noun and as a verb.

	NOUN ○	VERB
1. plant		
2. bark		
3. leaves		

Module 8 • Week 2

Authors tell events or steps in the order they happen.

✏ Number the steps in *PB & J Hooray!* in the order that they happen from 1 (first) to 5 (last).

✏ Draw a picture to show each step.

	People make and eat PB & Js!	
	Bakeries bake, factories make.	
	Trucks deliver ingredients from the bakeries and factories to the store.	
	Seeds are planted, crops grow.	
	People buy ingredients from the store.	

We read about how vegetables go from seed to soup! What do you need to grow and make vegetable soup?

Draw a picture of the things you need to grow and make vegetable soup.

Add labels to tell the names of the things.

Some words have more than one meaning.

 Listen to each sentence.

Draw a picture to show the meaning of the underlined word.

wave

slide	
1. I **slide** into the water.	2. The playground **slide** is green.

point	
3. The **point** of my pencil is sharp.	4. I **point** at the dog.

The **author's purpose** for writing a text can be to **persuade**, to **inform**, or to **entertain**. The author uses **words and pictures** to help persuade, inform, or entertain the reader.

✔ Check the author's purpose for writing *Rainbow Stew*.

☐ **Persuade**   ☐ **Inform**   ☐ **Entertain**

✏️ Write or draw things the author did to make the story fun.

💬 Tell your partner about how the author uses words and pictures to make the story fun.

Grandpa and the kids love to make his famous Rainbow Stew.
What is your favorite food to make?

Write your favorite food to make.

_____

- -

_____

Draw or write the steps that tell how you make
the food.

First,	Next,

Then,	Last,

MULTIPLE-MEANING WORDS

Some words have more than one meaning.
We can look up word meanings in a dictionary.

wave

🔍 Look up both meanings of each word in a dictionary.

👂 Listen to each sentence. Decide if the <u>underlined</u> word is a noun or a verb.

⭕ Circle **noun** or **verb**.

ship	
1. The **<u>ship</u>** sails in the ocean. noun verb	2. The factory will **<u>ship</u>** jelly to stores. noun verb

whistle	
3. I **<u>whistle</u>** to my dog. noun verb	4. The coach's **<u>whistle</u>** is shiny. noun verb

brush	
5. I **<u>brush</u>** my teeth. noun verb	6. The paint **<u>brush</u>** is clean. noun verb

Key details are facts or examples that give information about the central idea. Think about what you need to know to identify the most important details.

✏️ Draw or write two key details that support the central idea in *Why Living Things Need Homes*.

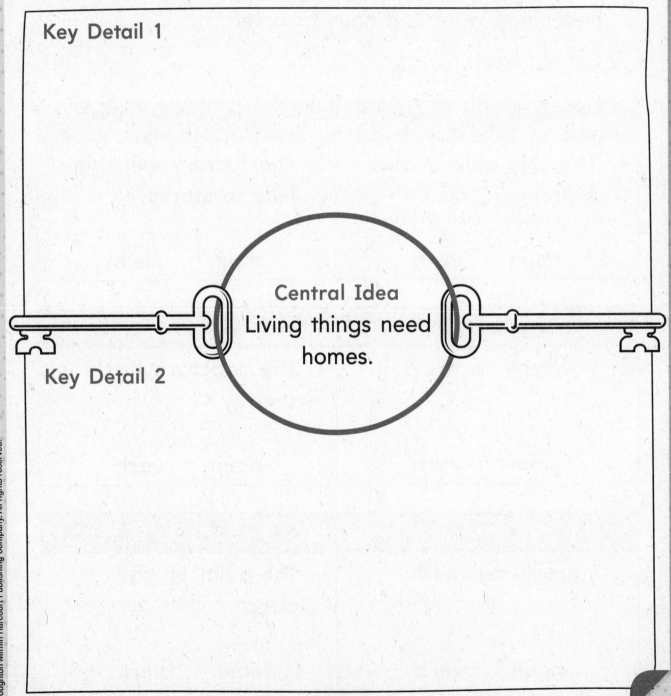

Key Detail 1

Key Detail 2

Central Idea
Living things need homes.

Animals live in habitats that are perfect for them! What is your favorite animal and what habitat does it live in?

Draw a picture of the animal in its habitat.

Write a sentence to tell which animal you chose and what habitat it lives in.

I am a _____

I am in _____

Use Big Idea Words to talk and write about a topic.

✔ Pick one sentence.

☐ A bird's **habitat** is ____.

☐ I wear ____ to **protect** me when I ride a bicycle.

☐ A tree can **provide** ____.

provide

✎ Draw a picture to show your response.

The **setting** is where and when a story takes place. Think about ideas from different parts of a text and put them together to form a new idea.

Write why each habitat is wrong for Bear.

_____

Underground: _____

Ocean: _____

Desert: _____

Put it together! Draw Bear's perfect habitat.

We learned all about black bears in *Black Bears*. What are three new facts you learned about black bears?

Write three facts about black bears.

Draw a picture for each fact.

Fact 1	

Fact 2	

Fact 3	

SORTING AND GROUPING

We can sort words and objects into groups.

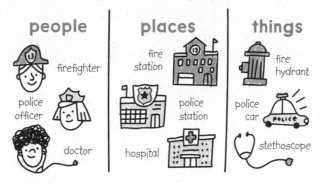

people	places	things
firefighter	fire station	fire hydrant
police officer	police station	police car
doctor	hospital	stethoscope

✏️ Color the animals that live in the water.

✏️ Draw a line from animals that live in the water to the water habitat.

camel

whale

tiger

octopus

water habitat

sea otter

bear

clown fish

MAKE CONNECTIONS

Think about ideas from different parts of a text and put them together to form a new idea.

Draw how each animal survives in the desert.

Desert Tortoise   Antelope
                    Ground Squirrel   _____

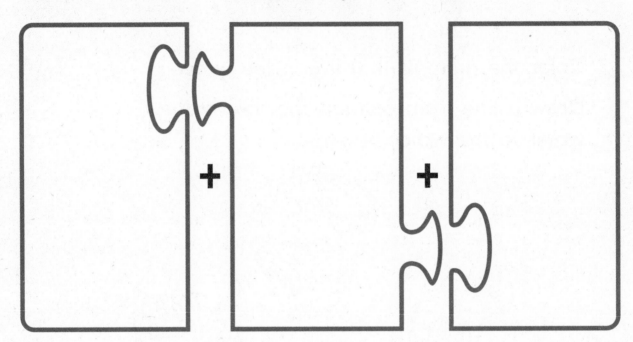

Put it together! How do animals survive in the desert?

=

Follow the pattern of *In the Tall, Tall Grass* to write about another animal.

Write two sounds the animal makes.

_____   _____

- - - - - - - - - - - - - - - - -   - - - - - - - - - - - - - - - - -

_____ ,   _____

Write the animal's name.

_____

- -

_____

Write an action that the animal does.

_____

- -

_____

Draw a picture of the animal in its habitat.

SORTING AND GROUPING

We can sort words and objects into groups.

people	places	things

 firefighter

police officer

doctor

 fire station

police station

hospital

 fire hydrant

police car

stethoscope

🔍 Look at the pictures. What groups can you make?

✏️ Write a group name at the top of each box.

✏️ Sort the things that live in the desert into groups.

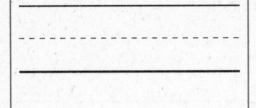
peccary

bluebonnet

cactus

jackrabbit

roadrunner

Module 9 • Week 3

PLOT: PROBLEM AND SOLUTION

The **problem** in a story is something that goes wrong or causes trouble. The **solution** is the way the problem is fixed or solved.

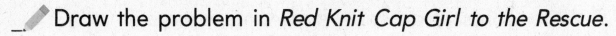 Draw the problem in *Red Knit Cap Girl to the Rescue.*

Problem

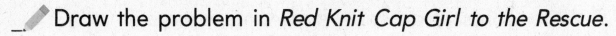 Draw the solution in *Red Knit Cap Girl to the Rescue.*

Solution

In *Polar Animals*, we read a poem that could've been written by a polar bear! Pretend you are an animal and write about yourself.

Write words to describe and name your animal.

_____

- -

I have _____
(animal feature)

_____

- -

I live in _____
(animal habitat)

_____

- -

Who am I? _____
(animal name)

Draw a picture to go with your animal description.

SORTING AND GROUPING

We can sort words and objects into groups.

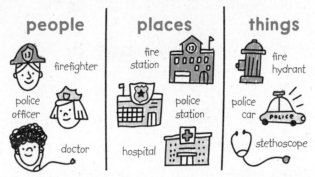

| people | places | things |

_ Look at the pictures and write a name for each group.

Color the pictures.

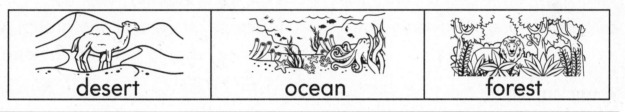

desert | ocean | forest

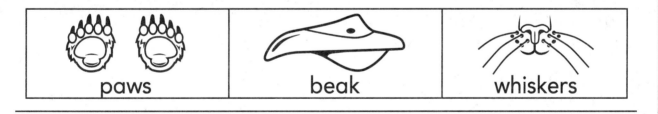

paws | beak | whiskers

Quack! | Moo! | Baa!

Glossary

Use the glossary to look up the meanings of words you don't know.

Aa

active (adjective)
When you are **active**, you move around a lot. *The children are active when they jump rope.*

allow (verb)
To **allow** something means to let it happen. *Using a pencil will allow you to erase when you're writing.*

America (noun)
America is another name for the United States. *My family lives in America.*

American (adjective)
Something or someone that is **American** has to do with the United States or its people. *The Statue of Liberty is an American symbol.*

anthem (noun)
An **anthem** is a song that is important to a certain place or group of people. *We sing an anthem about our school at the end of each day.*

Bb

believe (verb)
When you **believe** something, you think it is true. *I believe people should be nice to each other.*

belong (verb)
When you **belong**, you feel welcome as part of the group. *My coaches help me feel like I belong on the team.*

bloom (verb)
When plants or trees **bloom**, the flowers open up. *The cherry trees have beautiful pink flowers when they bloom.*

bother (verb)
To **bother** someone means to bug or upset someone. *My brother likes to bother me when I'm writing.*

brave (adjective)
Someone who is **brave** is not scared to do something. *The brave boy is ready to get a shot from the doctor.*

burrow (verb)
To **burrow** means to make a hole in the ground by digging. *The mole uses its long claws to **burrow** in the ground.*

burrow (noun)
A **burrow** is a hole in the ground that an animal makes to live in. *The rabbit's **burrow** has space for its whole family.*

busy (adjective)
If you are **busy**, you have lots of things to do. *My day is **busy**— after I'm done painting, I'm going to play soccer!*

Cc

care (verb)
If you **care** about something, you worry about what happens to it. *We **care** about our pet bunny so we take her to the veterinarian to make sure she is healthy.*

celebrate (verb)
When you **celebrate**, you do something fun to remember a special person or event. *Let's have a party to **celebrate** your birthday.*

change (verb)
To **change** something means to make it different. *Rainy weather can **change** my plans to play outside.*

cheer (verb)
When you **cheer**, you yell loudly to show that you like something. *We **cheer** for our favorite player when she throws the ball.*

city (noun)
A **city** is a place where many people live and work close together. *There are lots of people, buildings, and cars in the **city**.*

close (adjective)
When two things are **close**, they are near or next to each other. *The bears are **close** to the river.*

clue (noun)
A **clue** is information that helps you find something or solve a problem. *I looked closely for a **clue** to find the missing lunch box.*

community (noun)
A **community** is a group of people who live and work in the same place. *Everyone in our community went to see the parade.*

country (noun)
When you are in the **country**, you are far away from big towns and cities. *There are a lot of trees and fields in the country.*

country (noun)
A **country** is a place where all people live by the same rules. *Our country is the United States of America.*

crop (noun)
A **crop** is a plant that farmers grow to feed people. *One crop that many farmers grow is corn.*

crowd (noun)
A **crowd** is a group of people. *There is a large crowd of people watching the baseball game.*

curious (adjective)
When you are **curious**, you want to know or learn about new things. *The boys are curious about lizards, so they are reading a book to learn more about them.*

customer (noun)
A **customer** is someone who buys things. *The customer buys food at the store.*

Dd

decide (verb)
When you **decide**, you make a choice about something. *The girl needs to decide which fruit she wants to eat for snack.*

different (adjective)
If something is **different**, it is not the same. *The red flower is different from the others.*

disability (noun)
If you have a **disability**, you have something special about you that makes it hard to do certain things. *My friend has a disability, so he uses a wheelchair to move around the school.*

discover (verb)
When you **discover** something, you learn about it for the first time. *The girl will discover how caterpillars become butterflies.*

dream (noun)
A **dream** is something that you want or hope to do someday. *The girl's **dream** is to become a scientist.*

Ee

earn (verb)
If you **earn** something, you work hard to get it. *My brother rakes up leaves in the yard to **earn** money.*

encounter (verb)
If you **encounter** something, it means you see or experience it when you don't expect to. *The family was surprised to **encounter** some deer while on their walk.*

energized (adjective)
When you feel **energized**, you feel awake and ready to do things. *The children feel **energized** and want to play for hours.*

energy (noun)
When you have **energy**, you have the strength to move, play, and learn. *The children have a lot of **energy** to run and play.*

enormous (adjective)
Something that is **enormous** is very big. *An elephant is an **enormous** animal.*

exercise (verb)
When you **exercise**, you move your body to get strong. *I **exercise** every day by walking my dog.*

expect (verb)
If you **expect** something, you think it will happen. *I **expect** the bus will come soon because it's always on time.*

Ff

factory (noun)
A **factory** is a place where things are made. *The machine fills containers with orange juice in the **factory**.*

familiar (adjective)
When something looks **familiar**, it means that you have seen it before. *The people in the cafeteria are **familiar** to us because we see them every day!*

flow (verb)
To **flow** means to move along smoothly. *We let the river **flow** over our feet.*

forest (noun)
A **forest** is a large area covered with trees. *There are many trees and animals in the forest.*

free (adjective)
When something is **free**, it can do whatever it wants to do. *The ducks are free to swim around the pond.*

Gg

garden (noun)
A **garden** is a place to grow flowers, fruit, and vegetables. *He grows flowers in his garden.*

Hh

habitat (noun)
A **habitat** is a place where plants and animals live and grow. *The bear lives in a forest habitat with many tall trees.*

half (noun)
When you cut something in two pieces that are the same size, you cut it in **half**. *I cut the apple in half so we could share it.*

harvest (verb)
When you **harvest** foods, you pick and gather them. *I help harvest the vegetables that we grow.*

healthy (adjective)
Something that is **healthy** is good for your body. *He eats healthy food to keep his body strong.*

height (noun)
Your **height** is how tall you are. *The doctor checks my height during the appointment.*

help (verb)
When you **help**, you make it easier for someone to do something. *I like to help my mom with the laundry.*

hero (noun)
A **hero** is a person who does something brave to help others. *The firefighter is a hero because he helps people when their homes are on fire.*

hope (verb)
When you **hope** for something, you want it to happen. *I hope the plant grows flowers soon!*

Ii

idea (noun)
When you have an **idea**, you have a thought about what to do. *My friend has an idea for a new game to play.*

important (adjective)
If it is **important** for you to do something, it means you need to do it. *It is **important** to go to the dentist to get your teeth checked.*

ingredient (noun)
An **ingredient** is a food you use to make other foods. *One **ingredient** we always put in our salad is tomatoes.*

inspire (verb)
To **inspire** something means to cause it to happen or be created. *The stories **inspire** Sarah to want to travel to space.*

Jj

journey (noun)
A **journey** is a long trip. *Julian is excited for the **journey** to his grandpa's house.*

Ll

law (noun)
A **law** is a rule that all people must follow. *There is a **law** that you must wear your seatbelt when you are in the car.*

living (adjective)
Something that is **living** is alive. *Ducks are **living** things that can fly, swim, and walk.*

location (noun)
The **location** of something is where it is. *The **location** of my house is across the street from my school.*

lovely (adjective)
If something is **lovely**, it looks, sounds, smells, or feels nice. *The park has **lovely** flowers and trees.*

Mm

map (noun)
A **map** is a picture or drawing that shows streets, rivers, and other parts of a place. *We look at the **map** to see what roads to take on our trip.*

mistake (noun)
When you make a **mistake**, you do something the wrong way. *My teacher told me it's OK to make a **mistake** as long as I try hard.*

muscles (noun)
Your **muscles** are what move your body around. *She has strong **muscles** because she runs every day.*

Nn

neighbor (noun)
A **neighbor** is someone who lives near you. *My **neighbor** invited our family over for a barbecue.*

neighborhood (noun)
A **neighborhood** is a part of a city or town where people live. *We worked together to plant a garden in our **neighborhood**.*

Oo

observe (verb)
To **observe** something means to watch it closely and pay attention to it. *The girl stands nearby to **observe** the ducks.*

offer (verb)
When you **offer** something to someone, you let him or her have it. *It was nice of you to **offer** to share your cherries.*

ordinary (adjective)
If something is **ordinary**, it is normal and does not stand out. *I used an **ordinary** pencil to write my story.*

Pp

participate (verb)
To **participate** in an activity means to do an activity with others. *At the end of the school year, my friends and I **participate** in a tug of war.*

partners (noun)
Partners are people who work or play together. *The **partners** are reading together.*

peaceful (adjective)
If something is **peaceful**, it is calm and quiet. *Taking a walk in the woods can be **peaceful**.*

peel (verb)
When you **peel** something, you take off its skin. *We **peel** bananas before we eat them.*

plain (noun)
A **plain** is a flat piece of land with a lot of grass and only a few trees. *There are a few buffalo eating grass on the **plain**.*

plan (noun)
When you make a **plan**, you think about how to do something before you do it. *The girl made a **plan** to build a house for her toy dog.*

plant (verb)
To **plant** something means to put it in the ground so it will grow. *She will **plant** the beans so they will grow.*

polite (adjective)
If you are **polite**, you are kind to others and have good manners. *The boy is **polite** and says thank you when a friend gives him the art supplies.*

practice (verb)
When you **practice** something, you do it over and over again to get better. *The boy will **practice** tying his shoes until he can do it himself.*

prey (noun)
An animal that other animals hunt is the **prey**. *The bear caught its **prey**—a fish!*

pronounce (verb)
To **pronounce** a word means to say it in the correct way. *When I read a book aloud, I try to **pronounce** each word carefully.*

protect (verb)
To **protect** something, you keep it safe. *The turtle has a hard shell to **protect** its body.*

proud (adjective)
If you feel **proud** of yourself, you are happy with something you did that took hard work. *The girl is **proud** because she solved a math problem.*

provide (verb)
If you **provide** something, you give what is needed to live. *The momma bird catches a worm to **provide** food for the baby bird.*

puzzled (adjective)
If you are **puzzled**, you are not sure what to do. *The girl is **puzzled** by the game she is playing.*

Rr

real (adjective)
If something is **real**, it is not fake or made-up. *I can't believe I saw a **real** spider in its web!*

reflection (noun)
The image you see in a mirror and sometimes in water or glass is a **reflection**. *Kai looked at his **reflection** in the bathroom mirror.*

refuse (verb)
If you **refuse** to do something, you will not do it. *I am full after eating dinner, so I **refuse** to eat the dessert.*

relax (verb)
When you **relax**, you spend time lying down or doing something you enjoy. *It's nice to relax in a soft, comfortable chair.*

relaxing (adjective)
When something is **relaxing**, it helps calm your body and your mind. *Reading quietly can be very relaxing.*

research (verb)
To **research** means to look for information that answers questions about a topic. *We took books out from the library to research information for our project.*

respectful (adjective)
Someone who is **respectful** is polite and kind to others. *The children are respectful and raise their hands before talking.*

rest (noun)
Rest is a time when you sleep or do nothing after being active. *It's important to get enough rest at night so you feel ready for the day.*

right (noun)
A **right** is something that a person is allowed to do. *In the United States, children have the right to go to school.*

root (noun)
A **root** is part of a plant that grows underground and takes in water and food. *The orange part of a carrot is the root of the plant.*

row (noun)
A **row** is a straight line of things that are next to each other. *She plants the seeds in a row.*

Ss

safe (adjective)
If you are **safe**, you will not be hurt. *Jonathan wears a helmet to be safe while riding his bike.*

same (adjective)
When two things are the **same**, they are alike in every way. *My cousin and I have the same shoes.*

scared (adjective)
When you are **scared**, you are afraid of something. *I was scared by my friend's spider, even though it was fake.*

sea (noun)
The **sea** is a huge, salty body of water. *Many fish, whales, and other animals live in the sea.*

search (verb)
To **search** means to try to find something by looking carefully. *I had to search for my missing stuffed bunny all morning before I found it!*

seed (noun)
A **seed** is a small, hard part of a plant that can grow into a new plant. *Be careful when you eat watermelon so you don't eat a seed!*

serve (verb)
To **serve** food means to give it to someone to eat. *My mom and dad serve the food at dinner.*

serving (noun)
A **serving** is an amount of a food or a drink for one person. *We each have a serving of carrots and a serving of peas on our plates.*

several (adjective)
If you have **several** things, you have more than two but not many. *The girl is holding several crayons.*

share (verb)
When two people **share** something, they both have or use it. *It is nice to share toys with your friends.*

shell (noun)
The **shell** of an animal is the hard covering on the outside of its body that protects it. *A snail can hide in its shell if it senses danger.*

soil (noun)
Soil is the dirt that plants grow in. *My grandma and I planted vegetables in the soil.*

special (adjective)
Something is **special** if it is different from others. *A peacock is special because it has colorful feathers.*

spy (verb)
When you **spy** something, you see or find it. *The girl looks closely to spy the spots on the bug.*

steep (adjective)
When something is **steep**, it is almost straight up and down. *The steep mountain trail is hard to climb.*

stretch (verb)
When you **stretch**, you spread out your arms, legs, or body as far as you can. *The children stretch their arms and legs before playing a game.*

stripe (noun)
A **stripe** is a long, thin line. It can be in a different color than the parts next to it. Many **stripes** together can make a pattern. *I wore blue pants with a white stripe down the side of each leg.*

stuck (adjective)
When you are **stuck**, you can't think of what to do next. *The boy is stuck because he doesn't know what move to make next in the game.*

study (verb)
When you **study** something, you look at it closely to learn about it. *I will study the flower to learn about its different parts.*

sturdy (adjective)
When something is **sturdy**, it is strong and solid. *The bookshelves at the library are sturdy and can hold many books.*

success (noun)
If you have **success** with something you try, it means you do it well. *The girl is having success with hula-hooping—she is learning to do it well.*

surprise (noun)
A **surprise** is something you did not know you would see or do. *It was a surprise that my cousin was coming hiking with us!*

Tt

take care (verb)
When you **take care** of something, you make sure to keep it safe and healthy. *I will take care of my teeth by brushing them two times a day.*

team (noun)
A **team** is a group of people who play or work together. *Our baseball team won the game today!*

together (adverb)
When people do things **together**, they do them with each other. *The friends love to play soccer together.*

Uu

underground (adverb)
When something is **underground**, it is below the ground. *A groundhog lives **underground** in a safe home.*

Vv

variety (noun)
When you have a **variety** of something, you have different kinds of the same thing. *My salad has a **variety** of fruits in it.*

vine (noun)
A **vine** is a plant that has very long stems and that grows on the ground or up a wall. *Watermelons grow on a long **vine**.*

visit (verb)
To **visit** someone means to go see them. *We like to **visit** our grandparents.*

Ww

watch (verb)
When you **watch** something, you look at it and pay close attention. *I will **watch** the birds to see how they build their nest.*

weather (noun)
The **weather** describes what the air is like outside. *The **weather** can be sunny or rainy.*

weight (noun)
Weight is how heavy a person or thing is. *The doctor checks Andre's **weight**.*

wish (noun)
When you make a **wish** for something, you really want it to happen. *For my birthday, my biggest **wish** is to get a puppy!*

witness (noun)
A **witness** is a person who sees something and can tell about it. *My mom was a **witness** to the dog taking food off the counter.*

wonder (verb)
When you **wonder** about something, you want to learn more about it. *I **wonder** what makes fireflies glow.*

wonderful (adjective)
Something that is **wonderful** is very good. *Everyone likes Samuel's **wonderful** artwork.*

world (noun)
World is another word for the Earth, the place we all live. *People live in many different places around the* **world**.

worried (adjective)
If you are **worried**, you are afraid something bad might happen. *My brother is* **worried** *the game might get canceled because of the rain.*

Yy

young (noun)
An animal's **young** are its babies. *Puppies are a dog's* **young**.

Credits